What Is Biblical
Preaching?

Basics of the Reformed Faith

Also available in the series:

What Is Biblical Preaching?

ERIC J. ALEXANDER

P&R
P U B L I S H I N G
P.O. BOX 817 • PHILLIPSBURG • NEW JERSEY 08865-0817

Page design by Tobias Design

Printed in the United States of America

Library of Congress Cataloging-in-Publication Data

Alexander, Eric J.
  What is biblical preaching? / Eric J. Alexander.
    p. cm. — (Basics of the reformed faith)
  ISBN 978-1-59638-113-1 (pbk.)
  1. Preaching. 2. Bible—Homiletical use. I. Title.
  BV4211.3.A423 2008
  251—dc22

                    2008023722

INTRODUCTION

I suppose almost all of us who are called to preach have a deep-seated reluctance to speak or write about preaching, lest it seem we are in some sense satisfied with our own preaching. At the outset, I must disabuse you of any notion that I am even remotely satisfied with my preaching: quite the reverse is the case. Nor do I entertain any delusion that I have expertise on this subject.

However, I think this is in no sense inconsistent with having, as I do, the deepest possible conviction about, and a God-given burden for, the centrality of biblical preaching in the church today. As I write in the year 2008, I see no more urgent priority than to summon the church to a restoration of the place biblical, expository preaching apparently occupied in the apostolic resolve of Acts 6:4. I pray daily for its increase, and would do anything to encourage and stimulate true biblical preaching.

This material was first given at a conference of ministers in Toronto, Canada. It was rewritten when I had the privilege of delivering the Mair Lectures in the Faculty of Divinity at the University of Glasgow. To both audiences, I am deeply grateful for the warmth of their reception.

The aim of these lectures and this booklet is the same: to clarify in eight propositions the priority and essentials of biblical preaching. To these propositions I now turn:

- Biblical Preaching Is Fundamental in Its Importance
- Biblical Preaching Is Spiritual in Its Essence
- Biblical Preaching Is Didactic in Its Nature
- Biblical Preaching Is Expository in Its Form
- Biblical Preaching Is Systematic in Its Pattern
- Biblical Preaching Is Pastoral in Its Concern
- Biblical Preaching Is Clear in Its Structure
- Biblical Preaching Is Relevant in Its Application

BIBLICAL PREACHING IS FUN-DAMENTAL IN ITS IMPORTANCE

Some years before he died, Dr. W. E. Sangster, leading figure of Methodism in Britain, and minister of the Westminster Central Hall in London, confessed to a conference of ministers assembled in his church, "I long to go into every manse and vicarage in the land and confront men in the ministry with this question: 'Do you really believe in preaching as the primary means by which God brings men to salvation, and therefore as your primary task, to the accomplishment of which you will devote your best hours and your greatest energies?' " He would have wanted to do that even more urgently today, when there is such widespread doubt about the validity, and even about the relevance, of a preaching ministry. That crisis of confidence in preaching is of course not a modern phenomenon. Indeed the rises and falls of the church's history are really a reflection of the presence or absence of faithfulness and power in the pulpit. Times of reformation and revival are marked by a rediscovery of the priority of preaching. That is illustrated as early as the beginning of Samuel's ministry in Israel. We are told in 1 Samuel 3:1 that "in those days the word of the LORD was rare," and by the end of that chapter we find that "the LORD continued to appear at Shiloh, and there he revealed himself to Samuel through his word" (v. 21). Significantly, the next words in that passage are, "And Samuel's word came to all Israel" (4:1).

In our own generation, it is not difficult to see that there are a number of factors which have increased the lack of confidence in preaching.

Undoubtedly some are sociological. People like Marshall McLuhan have told us that we live in a "non-literary, non-community, TV, instant-tell, man-in-a-hurry age." In such an age, the sermon and its form are thought to be one of the vestigial remains of an interesting but irrelevant past.

Another reason is probably intellectual: the modern dislike of dogmatism. Authoritative proclamation in the present intellectual climate is something with which people are uncomfortable. ("My opinion is as good as his.") The relativist and subjectivist moods in modern thinking make dialogue seem a humbler and more democratic approach.

However, we must never forget that *exousia* is a New Testament concept, behind which lies the fact that ultimate authority belongs to God, and that he mediates that authority through his Word. So the true picture in the New Testament is not that of a congregation under the authority of the preacher; but of both preacher and congregation under the authority of God's written Word. Indeed, it seems to me that the fundamental place of preaching in the church is simply a corollary of the fundamental place of Scripture in the church. If you erode the latter, you will certainly erode the former. Church history has consistently demonstrated this. To be logical and consistent, if we say that Scripture is fundamental to the church's life and continuance, then it is the exposition of Scripture which is fundamental to the church's pattern of activity.

This whole issue of the authority of Scripture is quite crucial for our thinking about preaching, and not only in the sense of its authority as the inspired and inerrant Word that God himself has spoken. Undoubtedly if you destroy that conviction you will destroy so much that is essential in biblical preaching. But I think in the contemporary climate one of the most pressing issues is the doctrine of the *sufficiency* of Scripture. The issue is, is Scripture sufficient for all our needs in the life and witness of the church of Jesus Christ? A resounding "yes" to that question is the conviction which lies behind expository preaching. True expository preaching should itself be a testimony to the authority and sufficiency of Scripture for the church.

It is here that "the current cult of spontaneity," as J. I. Packer calls it, militates against true preaching. "Charismatic 'prophecy' (that is unpremeditated applicatory speech, uttered in God's name) is an extreme form of this," he writes, "but wherever interest centres on spontaneity rather than on substance, and passion in speakers is valued above preparation, true preaching must of necessity languish."[1]

To drive home the truth of the priority of preaching in the church, John Stott quotes two great Scotsmen of the late nineteenth century: first Alexander Whyte, who encouraged a Methodist minister with these words: "Never think of giving up preaching! The angels around the throne envy you your great work." And secondly, Peter Taylor Forsyth, outstanding theologian and native of Aberdeen, who began his book *Preaching and the Modern Mind* with this statement: "It is perhaps an overbold beginning, but I will venture to say that with its preaching, Christianity stands or falls."[2]

Now let me set out what I consider to be the main aspects of the biblical and theological evidence for the fundamental place of preaching in the Christian church.

The Biblical Evidence

The example of Jesus and the apostles is very clearly one of a teaching, preaching ministry. At the opening of his ministry in Nazareth, Jesus says, "The Spirit of the Lord is upon me, because he has anointed me to preach good news" (Luke 4:18). He then goes on to expound the relevance of that passage which he has been reading from Isaiah 61 within the context of the synagogue service. Thereafter, he goes about all Galilee teaching in the synagogues and preaching the gospel of the Kingdom. The demands of the crowd do not divert him. "Everyone is looking for you," they say after the healings at Capernaum; but Jesus says, "Let us go somewhere else—to the nearby villages—so I can preach there also. That is why I have come" (Mark 1:38).

His commission to the Twelve in Luke 9 and to the Eleven in Matthew 28 is primarily concerned with preaching the gospel. When we turn to the apostolic pattern, we find that the apostles are under a constraint to observe the dominical priority of preaching in the early church. Attempts to stop them lead to united earnest prayer in Acts 4, and to deliberate reorganization of structures in order to allow the ministry of the Word and prayer to become primary in Acts 6.

We need to remind ourselves that the book of Acts bears witness not only to the power of the Holy Spirit at work in the early church, but to the primary place of preaching in a Spirit-filled ministry.

The Theological Evidence

Behind the proposition that preaching is fundamental in the church's task, lie some quite basic theological facts.

One is the very nature of divine truth: it is not to be sought through discussion and dialogue. It is not arrived at through a synthesis of opinions. It has once-for-all been revealed, delivered, and committed to the church. In other words, it is a gospel. It is news and must be proclaimed and taught from the one authoritative source where God has given us that revelation, which is Holy Scripture. This is why the monologue character of preaching is inevitable. It is frequently derided, but it is derided because people do not understand the theological implications behind this. Monologue is of the essence of preaching, for the simple reason that we are speaking about a revelation that only God can give and which he has given to us in his Word in a one-directional way.

Another of the basic theological facts which confronts us is the nature of man as a fallen creature. In 2 Corinthians 4, Paul acknowledges that the mind of the natural man is blinded by the god of this world, so that he cannot see the glory of the gospel. That is his native condition. Now what is Paul's method of dealing with the darkened minds of men and women? His answer is in 2 Corinthians 4:2, "We have renounced secret and shameful ways; we do not use deception, nor do we distort the word of God. On the contrary, by setting forth the truth plainly we commend ourselves to every man's conscience in the sight of God."

So Paul faces the darkened mind of unregenerate man by spreading out the truth before him. His only hope is that the same God who commanded the light to shine out of darkness (at creation) will shine into his heart to give the light of the knowledge of the glory of God in the face of Christ (2 Cor. 4:6). And the means God uses to dispel that darkness is the plain setting forth of his truth. This is where the new creation begins.

It is so easy for this fundamental place of a straightforward biblical preaching ministry to be eroded. One Sunday evening some years ago, a student telephoned me from an English city where he was at University. "I have just traveled from the opposite side of this city back to my lodgings," he said. "I have been around almost every church which I have been told is evangelical in this city. I have heard some marvelous music. I have listened to scintillating dialogues. I have seen drama and dancing. I have been at all manner of different forms of worship. Many kindnesses have been extended to me. But I am here in my lodgings on this Sunday evening asking, 'Will nobody in this great city feed my soul?'" I believe there are far more people echoing that cry than we understand. And the really serious thing about it is that the erosion of a biblical, expository ministry is followed by the dilution of quality in Christian character and commitment.

So a biblical, preaching ministry is fundamental in its importance.

BIBLICAL PREACHING IS SPIRITUAL IN ITS ESSENCE

This is one of the most vital truths about biblical preaching. Let me explain what I mean: the task of true preaching is not essentially intellectual or psychological or rhetorical; it is essentially spiritual.

Left to ourselves, we may do many things with a congregation. We may move them emotionally. We may attract them to ourselves personally, producing great loyalty. We may persuade them intellectually. We may educate them in a broad spectrum of Christian truth. But the one thing we can never do, left to ourselves, is to regenerate them spiritually and change them into the image of Jesus Christ, to bear his moral glory in their character. While that is the great calling of the church of Christ, it is essentially God's work and not ours.

So it is possible to be homiletically brilliant, verbally flu-
ent, theologically profound, biblically accurate and orthodox,
and spiritually useless. That frightens me. I hope it frightens
you, too. I think it is of this that Paul is speaking when he says,
"I planted the seed, Apollos watered it, but God made it grow.
So neither he who plants nor he who waters is anything, but
only God, who makes things grow" (1 Cor. 3:6-7). It is very
possible for us to be deeply concerned about homiletical abil-
ity and fluency and theological profundity and biblical ortho-
doxy, but to know nothing of the life-giving power of God with
the burning anointing of the Holy Spirit upon our ministry.
Campbell Morgan (Lloyd-Jones's predecessor at the Westminster Chapel) divulged that at one crucial stage in his ministry
he was in precisely this position, and sensed that God was saying to him, "Preach on, great preacher, without me." Alan Red-
path used to say that the most penetrating question you could
ask about any church situation was, "What is happening in this
place that cannot be explained in merely human terms?"

So there is a world of difference between true biblical
preaching and an academic lecture or a rhetorical performance.
We are utterly dependent on the grace and power of the Holy
Spirit. Thank God, he uses the weak things of this world to con-
found the mighty, and the things that are not to bring to nothing the things that are (1 Cor. 1:28). This is why it is absolutely
essential to marry prayer to the ministry of the Word. In our
ministries prayer is not supplemental; it is fundamental.

Of course we subscribe to the principal that "this work is
God's work, not ours." We subscribe to that because we are
biblical Evangelicals, but the logical corollary of that statement is that prayer is a fundamental issue in the ministry of
the Word, as in every part of our labor, and not, as we tend to
make it, a supplemental matter.

E. M. Bounds, who wrote the remarkable little booklet
Power through Prayer, says, "The church is on a stretch if not on
a strain, looking for better methods. But men are God's meth-

ods and while the church is looking for better methods, God is looking for better men."[3]

That, of course, does not mean that we should not be interested in methodology. Nor does it mean that we have to be stupid enough to ignore new ideas and new insights, or to be careless in our administration and exploration of methods that are valuable and effective. But we do need to ask God to write on our hearts that this task he has given us is spiritual in its essence.

BIBLICAL PREACHING IS DIDACTIC IN ITS NATURE

By that I mean that we are called primarily to be *teachers* of the truth of God's Word. Our ultimate concern, of course, is to reach the heart and the will, but the scriptural route to the heart and to the will is through the mind. It is a very important thing for us to grasp this. This is undoubtedly the pattern of biblical preaching. Professor James S. Stewart wrote in his little book *Heralds of God*, "If it is bad to preach over people's heads, not to preach to their heads at all is worse."[4]

If you look at the language of Paul's preaching, it is the language of reasoning, persuading, and arguing. Significantly, the human response is frequently spoken of in terms of "being persuaded" (Acts 17:4). Or it is believing the truth (2 Thess. 2:13), acknowledging the truth (2 Tim. 3:7), or obeying the truth (Gal. 5:7).

Professor Donald Macleod of the Free Church College in Edinburgh has written this: "Evangelism as defined in Scripture, is a battle for the mind. Its very essence is the affirmation and explanation of truth, that is it needs to have a teaching content."[5]

William M. Taylor in his book *The Ministry of the Word* has a strong statement to the same effect: "To call upon

men constantly to come to Christ and to repeat perpetu-
ally the words of Paul to the jailer, 'Believe on the Lord
Jesus Christ,' without at the same time telling them who
Jesus Christ is and what it is to come to Him, is the merest
mockery. It is using the name of Christ as though it were
some cabalistic charm and reducing the Gospel message
to an empty formula. If therefore we would be effective
evangelists, we must be ready to give an answer to him
who asks us, 'Who is this Jesus that I may believe on him?
What is there in His dying that has any relation to me?'"[6]

Now I believe that to be of great importance. Of
course it is true that Scripture summons us to call men to
decision. And it may have been an error of some that they
have omitted this thrust in the Scripture. But we need to
be sure that they know what they are deciding about. So
our preaching must have a teaching content, and the exposition of Scripture is the essence of that. It is significant that the old order of sin makes its appeal through the
senses and the appetite (Gen. 3:6), whereas the new order
in Christ makes its appeal through the mind and the understanding (Rom. 12:2).

BIBLICAL PREACHING IS EXPOSITORY IN ITS FORM

John Stott touches upon this theme very helpfully in
the third chapter of his book *I Believe in Preaching*. "It is
my contention that all true Christian preaching is expository preaching," he says, and then enlarges on the theme:
"The expositor prises open what appears to be closed,
makes plain what is obscure, unravels what is knotted and
unfolds what is tightly packed. The opposite of exposition
is 'imposition,' which is to impose on the text what is not
there. . . . In expository preaching, the Biblical text is neither a conventional introduction to a sermon on a largely

different theme, nor a convenient peg on which to hang a ragbag of miscellaneous thoughts, but a master which dictates and controls what is said."[7]

What that implies for us as preachers is that the quarry in which we work and from which we dig is the quarry of Holy Scripture. There is no other quarry from which we may find the gold of God's truth. To change the metaphor, the food we serve to people, the bread we break to them, is Holy Scripture. There is no other bread. The sword which we wield, to change the metaphor again, is the Word of God. *That* is the sword of the Spirit. We dare not put some other sword into the Spirit's hand and expect him to use it. The sword of the Spirit is the Word of God. We are therefore to preach the Word, which means preach the Scriptures: to devote ourselves (as Paul says to Timothy in 1 Tim. 4:13) to the public reading, preaching, and teaching of Scripture, correctly handling the Word of God.

The underlying reason for this exclusivity is that outside Holy Scripture, we have no authoritative Word from God. With the eroding of confidence in the authority of Scripture in our own generation, it is not at all surprising that there has been an evacuation of authority from the pulpit. The decline in preaching is almost inevitably a result of such an absence of conviction concerning the authority of Scripture. The history of the Christian church bears ample and sad testimony to this connection.

The whole cast of a truly biblical ministry will be a concern that people should recognize our only interest is not in selling our own line, or persuading people of our own opinion, or seeking that they might adopt our own view on a particular issue, but in humbly, obediently, and openly seeking to deal with what Holy Scripture says, opening it up and making it plain. The task has never been more clearly illustrated than in the ministry of Nehemiah in Nehemiah 8 where the people are met together under the Word of God. The ministry which the Levites fulfilled was to "read from the book of the Law of God, making it clear and giving the meaning so that the people could understand what was being read" (Neh. 8:8).

Our calling as Christian preachers is to follow that example, taking the Word of God and exposing its truth and teaching it in all its inexhaustible depth. Ultimately, this is the answer to the complaint of a young man I met at a conference in England years ago. "I have exhausted everything I could think of in my preaching. I am now barren and without material. I am like a dried-up spring." Now what he had been almost universally advised to do was to move from this parish to another. The reason for his problem became obvious as he enlarged upon it to me. "One of my greatest difficulties is not so much preparing the material but after I have done so finding a text in the Bible that will fit the theme." The man had clearly not been preaching the Bible. His only use of Scripture was to make it a launching pad from which he would take off into a sphere where he would preach on a subject unrelated to his text. The Scripture, however, is not *our* servant, so that we use it to say something we want to say. Rather we are Scripture's servants to allow Scripture to say through us what God has said. That is where true exposition demands of us total integrity with the text of the Bible. I may not say everything that is in the text, but by the grace of God I will want to say nothing that is contrary to the text. That kind of integrity is intrinsic to true biblical preaching.

I think the expository task involves at least the following elements:

Prolonged Meditation on the Passage or Text of Scripture

It is important for us to have a clear doctrine of illumination as well as a clear doctrine of revelation. We are dependent on God as much for illumination as we are for revelation. Revelation is the objective emphasis in our doctrine of Scripture. Illumination is the subjective emphasis. The primary way in which God illumines the truth of Scripture to us is through prolonged meditation upon it. This is what Paul is instructing Timothy in, when he says in 2 Timothy 2:7, "Think over what I say, for the Lord will give you understanding in everything" (ESV).

Therefore, in preparation the preacher should not make a dash to his commentaries first of all, but should meditate on the content of the passage, ruminating on its truth, pondering the meaning, and all the time calling upon God to enlighten his understanding and give him wisdom and grace to grasp the truth that is here written. Psalm 119 is full of this spirit: "Give me understanding" (v. 34), "My eyes stay open through the watches of the night, that I may meditate on your promises" (v. 148), "The unfolding of your words gives light; its gives understanding to the simple" (v. 130).

One of my own idiosyncrasies was that I used to record the passage that I was preaching on or expounding and then, when I had a car journey, I played the tape in the car. The tape would stop when the speaking stopped and then go back to the beginning again. Thus I had this particular passage played again and again in my ears, and insights would dawn on me. If these insights were significant I would record them on my pocket dictating machine.

Thorough Exegesis

I am referring now to the painstaking process of using all the tools that God has given us and whatever gifts he may have entrusted to us, in a careful study of the passage or text. At this point we will be asking, "What precisely does the writer say?" To answer this question we will be taking up such lexicons, dictionaries, and whatever other tools of that kind we may have or have access to. We will be interested in the shades of meaning of words, the grammatical construction of tenses, and so on. Over the years the International Critical Commentary has been the stock in trade of exegetes, but there are more modern ones. The New International Commentaries on the Old Testament and New Testament (published by Eerdmans) are particularly helpful.

Careful Interpretation

The question with which we are dealing here is not just, "What did the writer say?" but, "What does he mean, and what does this mean for us today?" Now, here the Westminster Confession puts the main rule clearly in that rich and priceless section called "The Directory for the Public Worship of God." It says, "The infallible rule of interpretation of Scripture is the Scripture itself, and therefore when there is a question about the true and full sense of any Scripture, it must be searched and known by other passages that speak more clearly."

John Knox said the same thing in this way, "The Word of God is plain in itself and if there appear any obscurity in one place, the Holy Ghost, who is never contrarious with Himself, explains the same more clearly in another place."[8] The perspicuity of Scripture is an important doctrine for us to have constantly before us.

One of our most basic guidelines should certainly be that we interpret Scripture *contextually*. That simply means that we need to look at every Scripture in the light of the whole and at every smaller part in the light of the larger part. So the context of a word will be the sentence in which it occurs. The context of the sentence will be the verse, the context of the verse the chapter or passage, and the context of the chapter the book. But the context of the book is of course the whole Bible.

Faithful Exposition

Here we will be seeking to draw out the doctrine which this passage or text teaches and assemble it in such a way that it is teachable material. Exposition is not just a verse-by-verse commentary on the passage. Rather, we are seeking to crystallize the truth it sets forth and focus on the main message or point of the passage or text. People should then go away saying, "Ah, so that is what this passage of Scripture means; that is what it teaches; that is what God is saying here." One of the great tests of expository preaching is that people should be able to go back to the Scriptures when they are at home and dig out for themselves precisely what the preacher has dug out for them. This is the Berean approach, described for us in Acts 17:11. One of the things we should be doing in expository preaching is enabling people to study the Scripture for themselves. We should be showing them the way to feed themselves. Of course, some people may come back to you and say, "Now I am not at all sure if that is what this passage is saying." Then we preachers need to be humble enough to say, "Well, I am eager to learn. My only interest is to discover what Scripture is teaching."

There are two words used in the New Testament for exposition. One is the Greek word *ektithemi*, which is used four times—in Acts 7:21; 11:4; 18:26; and 28:23—and is often translated "explained." But really it has the idea of being taken out and exposed. The language does give us some insight into what true exposition means. For example, the use in Acts 7:21 in Stephen's speech refers to the whole idea of Moses' exposure, and it is highly instructive. The picture is of Moses being taken from the bulrushes at the age of three months and being exposed to the eyes of those who were present. The contents of this casket, which had such special treasure within it, were made visible for all to see. That is the picture of exposition; it is the exposure of the priceless content of Holy Scripture, so that people may say, "We had no idea that there was such treasure here." The other word is the Greek word *phaneroo* and the noun *phanerosis*, which Paul uses in 2 Corinthians 4:2-3. It means principally "unveiling" or "unravelling." Both ideas are of great importance for expository preaching and teaching. When a picture is unveiled publicly, there is really a double unveiling that needs to take place. In an art gallery when someone unveils a new painting, it is exposed to the public, but if you are like me, you will need someone to interpret the meaning of that artistic creation. So there is an objective and a subjective unveiling. The word *phanerosis* has also the idea of disentangling a tangled skein of wool. Again, we disentangle the truth to set it before people plainly.

It is, of course, through such a ministry that the preacher himself should grow in grace and grow in Christ and grow as a man and as a preacher. It is immensely important that through our own dealing with the Scriptures we ourselves should experience the impact of the truth. We need to experience God the Holy Spirit opening up this text to us so that it has sanctifying power in our own lives. In other words, we need to be exhibitors of the very thing we are aiming at in the lives of others.

It seems to me that this is at least part of the answer to the question preachers frequently face: "How do you feed your own soul? How do you avoid running dry yourself?" Such questions appear to ignore the obvious truth that when the Word of God grips your own soul and you are feeding upon it as you study, then there is bread for the sower as well as bread for the eater. It ought surely to be impossible for us to meditate on the Word of God and pour over its truth and pray out the meaning of it and yet be unblessed ourselves. The preacher must never be a mere academic when he is preparing to preach the Scriptures. Both in our ministry and in our personal lives, we need to bear witness to our deep confidence in the saving and sanctifying power of the Word of God. When Jesus prays in John 17:17, "Sanctify them by the truth. Your word is truth," he identifies the sanctifying instrument which God universally uses: that is, his Word.

That of course is not an automatic or mechanical thing. It needs to be married to prayer, both our own praying and the praying of the congregation. Congregations need to be taught their responsibility to pray out the bread of life for people. Do you remember the man who came to his friend at midnight and would not give him rest until he had found bread for his friends? That is a picture of the ministry which the people of God have. They are called to come before him and, as it were, to give him no rest until they have prayed out bread for others.

Now, such expository preaching does make great demands on time and energy. But this is where we need to work out our priorities and assess our commitment to the task. If indeed such preaching is the fundamental work of our ministry, we need to reassess our priorities and work out our timetables so that our best hours and our greatest energies are given to it. Bishop Ryle used to say, "There are no gains without pains." I think it was Dick Lucas who was asked by someone what was the secret of a fruitful ministry? His reply surprised those who stood around. He said simply, "Hard work."

BIBLICAL PREACHING IS SYSTEMATIC IN ITS PATTERN

I mean by that "systematic" as opposed to "haphazard," or "planned" as distinct from "unplanned." This can be accomplished, of course, in all sorts of ways. Consecutive exposition through a book, or through a well-defined part of a book, is probably the most satisfactory of these ways. Expository ministry should also be a systematic ministry. I think it needs to be done in a balanced and imaginative way, rather than a wooden and lopsided one. Particularly it needs to be balanced between Old Testament and New Testament, between gospel and epistle, between doctrinal and practical, and between historical and experimental.

Perhaps also, it needs to be imaginative and reasonable in the length of time we take for a series of expositions through a book. We need to be sensitive, both to the capacities of our people and to our own gifts in this connection. There is no doubt that one of the basic principles of faithful preaching in the context of a congregation is that we should preach to the people who are there, rather than to a congregation we would wish to be there. That is, you must know them, so that you know their needs, their capacities, their background, their present level of understanding, and so on. I am intrigued to know whether Charles Haddon Spurgeon's experience as a youngster put him off consecutive exposition for the rest of his life. Certainly something did! When he was a boy, he sat under the ministry of someone who, as he put it, droned on for years through the Epistle to the Hebrews. Spurgeon writes, "I do not know what this did to the Hebrews, but it sadly bored one Gentile lad." So, as far as we know, Spurgeon did not ever engage in consecutive exposition.

By contrast, Dr. Martyn Lloyd-Jones preached for fourteen years on the Epistle to the Romans, to the eternal blessing of those who heard these thrilling expositions. However, that is not a sufficient reason for most of the rest of us to preach similarly for fourteen years on the same book. The great advantage of expository ministry, going through a book of the Bible passage by passage, is that it disciplines us to cover topics and issues we might never otherwise have chosen to touch. Personally, I have found again and again that as I have come to a particular passage or chapter, I could not have begun to think of anything more relevant for a current situation in the congregation at that time. Now of course in a sense we should not be surprised at that, because we believe in a living God whose providential dealings with his people are experienced in this way.

One of the most important things to say about this whole question of systematic preaching, is what Dr. Lloyd-Jones emphasizes in chapter 10 of his remarkable book *Preaching and Preachers*. He warns us against the danger of rigidity. For example, there may be an occasion when you are in the midst of a series of expositions through a book, when the Holy Spirit grips your soul and presses upon you a particular message for a particular time or occasion. I agree entirely with Dr. Lloyd-Jones when he says that it would be foolish to ignore or dismiss that experience.

In this connection, another matter which is of great importance is that each sermon, even when you are preaching through a series, should be an entity in itself. You will almost never have exactly the same congregation on two consecutive Sundays and, depending on the nature of the church, there may be some who are visiting only for one Sunday. So we need to ensure that the sermon is complete in itself and has a climax of its own, and a thrust and application of its own.

BIBLICAL PREACHING IS PASTORAL IN ITS CONCERN

John Owen wrote that "the first and principal duty of a pastor is to feed the flock by diligent preaching of the Word. It is a promise relating to the New Testament, that God would give unto his church pastors according to His own heart, which should feed them 'with knowledge and understanding' (Jeremiah 3:15). . . . This feeding is of the essence of the office of a pastor, as unto the exercise of it; so that he who doth not, or can not, or will not, feed the flock is no pastor whatever outward call or work he may have in the church."[9] Owen answers the false dichotomy which is often drawn between the calling of the good pastor and the preacher. People often say, "Oh, he is not much of a preacher, but he is a great pastor." We ought, of course, never to divide the two. It is by faithful ministry of the Word of God that true pastoral care comes. We are to pastor biblically and to preach pastorally. It is significant that the apostle Paul describes himself in various roles in the one ministry: he is not only a herald of the gospel, and a custodian of the truth, and an expositor of Scripture; he is also a father to his children, a travailing mother who goes through the pain of bearing them, and a gentle nursemaid who learns loving patience with them.

All of these things ought to be visible in a truly biblical preaching ministry, because it is from Scripture that the pastoral model comes. This of course is just to say that we can never be detached from the people to whom we are ministering. A lecturer may be, but a preacher never can be. If we are truly undershepherds of the Chief Shepherd, we will find ourselves frequently within our own spirits calling, as we look out over the people, with the same concern that made the Chief Shepherd cry, "Oh Jerusalem, Jerusalem, you who kill the prophets and stone those sent to you, how often I have longed to gather your children together, as a hen gathers her chicks under her wings, but you were not willing" (Matt. 23:37).

This pastoral longing, this burden for the salvation of our people, this ache to see them shaped and molded into the image of Christ, and to see their rebellion changed into obedience: this is the essence of the pastor's heart. We dare not preach to people such truths as Holy Scripture contains, with a cold and clinical touch. True biblical preaching will not just be accurate, orthodox, thorough, biblical, and exegetical. It must also be warm, loving, full of grace as well as full of truth. If the Word of God brings chastening and rebuke, it needs to be done in the way a father would administer that to a child whom he loved earnestly. People need to be able to see that we care for them, more than we care for our own reputation as preachers. They need to know that what we say comes from the Word of God. But it is almost of equal importance that it evidently comes from our own hearts, and that, like the Chief Shepherd himself, we really would lay down our lives for their sake.

That, of course, implies that we will not simply preach to them. We will pray for them. Like the High Priest, their names will be carved into our hearts. It may seem like moving from the sublime to the ridiculous to say that that is one solution to the problem of remembering people's names. For the biblical preacher, the church roll is not primarily a location finder. It is primarily a prayer list.

BIBLICAL PREACHING IS CLEAR IN ITS STRUCTURE

This theme may not in fact be so far removed from the whole area of pastoral concern. If we truly care for people, we will want to break the bread of God down in such a way that they will find no unnecessary obstacles in digesting it.

I think the general principle in this whole matter of structure is that what is not clear to me before I begin to preach will certainly not be clear to anybody else after I have finished. We therefore need to strive for clarity.

I also tend to think that there is a theological reason behind this whole concept of structure. It is that God is a God of order, and not of chaos, and he has left the imprint of that in the universe. He is also a rational God, who reasons with his people in logical form, in order to persuade them. Perhaps one might say that Scripture itself bears the marks of its divine origin in this way amongst many others: it reveals both order and reason. And that, of course, is why the structure for which we will strive will most often be present in the text or passage itself.

Again, structure often appears after prolonged meditation. People used to say of Alexander McLaren, the great nineteenth-century biblical expositor, that he had a golden hammer with which he would tap a text and it fell into three divisions. However, it is much more likely that McLaren spent a great deal of time meditating on the text, and the structure and clarity of his address was the product of an enormous amount of hard work.

Of course, structure is not necessarily a series of headings: it can also be a series of logical arguments, as it is in so many of the Epistles. For example, in places like Romans 8, you find Paul asking a number of questions that follow on from each other and making statements that build upon each other. However we do it, I think we will discover that the vast majority of people need pegs on which to hang their thinking. We, on our part, need to take the time and trouble necessary to clarify the truth for them.

There are, however, two things we need to be warned about. The first is that the structure needs to represent the content of the text or passage. It must never be an ill-fitting box into which the truth is thrust, as if we were more concerned with the packaging than with the content. It is very easy for us to try to thrust the truth into headings that we think are particularly striking or well chosen. The structure must represent the truth within the text or passage. In this connection, such aids as alliteration must be servants and never masters.

Accepting these two caveats, we need to work hard at being clear.

A few years ago I was traveling on a plane, and my companion in the seat beside me had a fairly thorough glance at the books I was reading. I suppose they immediately identified the work in which I was engaged. He told me that he worshipped in a Presbyterian church every Sunday. It seemed too much of a coincidence not to tell him that I also was a Presbyterian and I was going to a seminary to speak to students for the ministry about preaching. He immediately began to give me some advice: "Do you know what I think is wrong with almost every preacher I hear? I think they spend most of their time preaching to one another and trying to impress one another. Now my dad used to tell me that if you wanted to hear the pure Christian gospel presented so that you would understand it you should go to a Presbyterian church service because that's what they did." Now I have no idea where that man went to church, but I do think that his criticism has at least some validity and should cause most of us preachers to say, "Ouch!" Bishop J. C. Ryle made frequent pleas to the clergy in his Diocese of Liverpool that they should "preach simply."

Apparently, John Wesley read his sermons to a simple, uneducated girl who acted as his maid. On Saturday evenings he asked her to stop him when there was something she could not understand or take in. His motive was a desire for clarity and simplicity.

BIBLICAL PREACHING IS RELEVANT IN ITS APPLICATION

I am told that someone said of Robert Murray McCheyne of Dundee, "He seemed, as his preaching progressed, to advance upon you until he was standing inside your heart, applying the Word of God to all your life."

My own increasing conviction is that this application begins again at our own door. I think the secret of applicatory preaching is that we must apply to ourselves the Word of God while we are meditating upon it, while we are studying it. We must do this before we ever begin to think about applying it to other people.

John Owen wrote, "A man preacheth that sermon only well unto others, which preacheth itself in his own soul. If the Word do not dwell with power in us, it will not pass with power from us."[10] And again, "He who doth not feed on and digest and thrive by what he preaches and prepares for his people, may give them poison as far as he knows, for unless he finds the power of it in his own heart, he cannot have any ground of confidence that it will have power in the hearts of others."[11]

Owen is speaking about applicatory preaching; that is, about applying the Word to our own lives. We will recognize the importance of this in our own experience. It is not that we preach our own experience. It is the truth of God in all its objective width and glory that we preach. But we must preach it as those who have experienced it, and know its power in our own lives, at least in some measure.

Of course that does not mean that we are to have the arrogance that would be able to say, "All that Holy Scripture teaches, I have myself experienced." That would never be a possibility. What it does mean, however, is that we are where the people are. We are with them in our concern that this Word may be applied to all of us. We must never hector them or lecture them as those who stand high above them. We are there with them under the Word of God. That is the real picture of biblical preaching. It is not the picture of people under the authority of the preacher; it is the preacher and the people under the authority of Holy Scripture. And that begins in the study. It is for this reason that we will find ourselves, whether physically or merely metaphorically, turning aside from our desk to our knees and crying to God, "Lord what does this mean for me? What duty is there here that I need to observe? What sin is there here that I need to forsake? What truth about my glorious Savior do I need to embrace for my well-being?" Then our preaching will be applicatory.

Now of course we will recognize and acknowledge that it is the Holy Spirit who is the true applier of the Word. That is a vital, central, basic truth for all our thinking. It is the Holy Spirit who takes the Word of God and uses it as the sword that pierces to the dividing asunder of soul and spirit. But that does not excuse us from the labor of asking, "How ought I to apply these truths to my own conscience and then to the conscience of this people?"

Let me quote to you from the Westminster Directory for Public Worship: "The preacher is not to rest in general doctrine, although never so much cleared and confirmed, but is to bring it home to special use by application to his hearers."

In the first section of this booklet, I said that an essential element in preaching was that it had a monologue character, and that this had a theological foundation in the fact that Scripture is revelation. Man is dead in trespasses and sins and darkened in his understanding, and the monologue character of Scripture and of preaching is an essential element in bringing him out of darkness into light, and out of confusion into the truth. We dare not apologize for that.

But it is also *dialogue* and it is important for us to see the sense in which that is true. It is not dialogue in the sense that I speak my part, somebody else speaks his, and by the process of synthesis we discover the truth. Dialogue is actually a Greek word used by Luke in Acts to describe Paul's preaching. It says he "dialogued with them." It means that he took the truth of the gospel and he dialogued with their minds concerning it. He would ask questions, for example. He spoke to them in this way: "Do you not know that your bodies are members of Christ himself?" (1 Cor. 6:15), "Do you not realize that Christ Jesus is in you?" (2 Cor. 13:5), "You were running well. Who hindered you?" (Gal. 5:7 ESV), "Who has bewitched you?" (Gal. 3:1). He brings logical arguments to bear upon them: "He who did not spare his own Son but delivered him up for us all, how will he not also with him graciously give us all things?" (Rom. 8:32 ESV).

Do you see what the apostle is doing? He is saying, "Think about this. Reason it out. If God has done the infinitely greater thing, will he not do all the lesser things? Can you possibly be afraid of being deprived of anything that will ever be good for you when he has given you his own Son?" In other words, he is dialoguing with their minds. And we should do exactly the same, applying the truth to people through their minds and calling upon them for a response. Above all, of course, it is the Holy Spirit who takes the Word of God and does this.

We are thus to be contemporary in our application. For that reason, it is important that we know the world and the pattern of thinking in the world in which we live. For that reason too it is important that we know the world in which our congregation lives. Evangelicals have traditionally been strongest in knowing the Scripture, and weakest in knowing the world. Others have mostly been stronger in knowing the world and weakest in knowing the Scripture. But there is no reason why these two things should be mutually exclusive.

"FINALLY, BRETHREN . . ."

Paul often uses this little phrase, perhaps to comfort the readers of his letters that there is not too much more to come. At other times, it may indicate that he is about to say the most important thing of all. I will leave you to judge which applies in this case!

What I want to say a little about is that mysterious, and yet real and glorious experience of God's Holy Spirit anointing the preacher in such a way that he finds himself almost a spectator of Another at work in the preaching of that sermon. It was of such an occasion Paul spoke when he recollects for the Thessalonians that "our gospel came to you not simply with words, but also with power, with the Holy Spirit and with deep conviction" (1 Thess. 1:5). It was of the preacher that someone said as we filed out after a remarkable Sunday service, "My, but the hand of God was upon that man this evening."

Our forefathers would have called this "the unction of the Holy Spirit." Charles Haddon Spurgeon wrote, "I wonder how long we might beat our brains before we could plainly put into words what is meant by preaching with unction. Yet he who preaches knows its presence, and he who hears soon detects its absence."[12] E. M. Bounds adds, "This unction is not the gift of genius. It is not found in the halls of learning. No eloquence can woo it. No industry can win it. No prelatical hands can confer it. It is Heaven's distillation in answer to prayer."[13]

When the unction of God is upon the preacher of his Word, people will go away saying, not "What a great preacher!" but rather, "Truly, God is in this place! How great and glorious he is!"

Some time ago, a young man who had recently been inducted to his first charge as a minister asked me, "What is the most important thing that I can do?" My immediate answer to him was, "Pray for a praying people."

Let me finally close with a more personal word. There is really nothing in the whole world quite like the labor of expository preaching. It is utterly consuming. It may sometimes be utterly exhausting, sometimes utterly exhilarating, but it is the most glorious privilege in all the world.

From time to time in the course of the years, I have found myself getting up from my study desk and walking around saying to myself, "Fancy being paid for doing this!" And when you think of it, that is one of the great mysteries of life, because to be entrusted with the exposition of the Word of God to his people is a privilege beyond understanding.

NOTES

1 James I. Packer, *Honouring the Written Word of God* (Carlisle, England: Paternoster, 1999), 250.

2 J. R. W. Stott, *I Believe in Preaching* (London: Hodder and Stoughton, 1982).

3 E. M. Bounds, *The Complete Works of E. M. Bounds* (Grand Rapids: Baker, 1990), 447.

4 James S. Stewart, *Heralds of God* (London: Hodder and Stoughton, 1946), 152.

5 Donald Macleod, "Preaching and Systematic Theology," in *The Preacher and Preaching*, ed. Samuel T. Logan Jr. (Phillipsburg, NJ: Presbyterian & Reformed, 1986), 261–62.

6 William M. Taylor, *The Ministry of the Word* (Nashville: Nelson, 1876), 83.

7 J. R. W. Stott, *I Believe in Preaching*, 125–26.

8 John Knox, *History of the Reformation in Scotland*, ed. William Croft Dickinson, 2 vols. (London: T. Nelson, 1949), 2:18.

9 John Owen, *The Complete Works of John Owen*, ed. William Goold, 16 vols. (London: Banner of Truth, 1966), 16:74.

10 Ibid., 11:76.

11 Ibid., 9:455.

12 C. H. Spurgeon, quoted in E. M. Bounds, *Power through Prayer* (London: Marshall Brothers, 1912), 87.

13 Ibid., 92–93.